THE ULTIMATE PEACE
America's Challenge in the Middle East

by Dr. Charbel E-H Moussa

DORRANCE PUBLISHING CO., INC.
PITTSBURGH, PENNSYLVANIA 15222

The contents of this work including, but not limited to, the accuracy of events, people, and places depicted; opinions expressed; permission to use previously published materials included; and any advice given or actions advocated are solely the responsibility of the author, who assumes all liability for said work and indemnifies the publisher against any claims stemming from publication of the work.

All Rights Reserved
Copyright © 2009 by Dr. Charbel E-H Moussa
No part of this book may be reproduced or transmitted in any form or by any means, electronic or mechanical, including photocopying, recording, or by any information storage and retrieval system without permission in writing from the publisher.

ISBN: 978-1-4349-0240-5
Library of Congress Control Number: 2008937094

Printed in the United States of America

First Printing

For more information or to order additional books, please contact:
Dorrance Publishing Co., Inc.
701 Smithfield Street
Pittsburgh, Pennsylvania 15222
U.S.A.
1-800-788-7654
www.dorrancebookstore.com

I would like to dedicate this book to my beloved wife, Dina; my parents, Therese and Michael; my brothers, Pierre and Maroun, and their families; and my sisters, Rosaline, Nancy, Rita, and Sylvana, and their families.

Contents

Part I 1

Foreword 3

Chapter I 8
Iran's Regional Role and U.S. Policy

Chapter II 16
Sunni and Shiite Muslims: A Never Ending Schism

Chapter III 25
Culture and Democracy

Chapter IV 34
September 11, 2001, and the Defeated Purpose

Chapter V 41
The Corruption of Ideas

Chapter VI 51
Democracy and Corporate Journalism

Part II 57

Chapter VII 59
The U.S. Role in Future Mideast Policies

Chapter VIII 65
A New Mediterranean

Chapter IX 71
Architecture of the New Mediterranean

Chapter X 79
Security and Strategic Co-operation

Chapter XI 87
Mediterranean Human Rights

Chapter XII 92
Education Is the Backbone of Development

Chapter XIII 100
The Environment and Natural Resources

Putting It in Perspective 109

Part I

FOREWORD

In the wake of the 9/11 terrorist attacks, U.S. President George W. Bush vowed to take the fight to the enemies and declared the world changed forever. The war on terror found strategic allies and attracted considerable criticism, while its course evolved into a war of ideologies and a struggle for (inter) national security. The destruction of the Taliban in Afghanistan brought a pro-U.S. government but drove Al-Qaeda underground, and Osama Bin Laden and his top lieutenants are yet to be found. The Iraq war took an entirely different outlook; it destroyed the Baath regime of Saddam Hussein and installed a Shiite dominant government that can neither be considered a friend nor an enemy of the U.S., while bringing out an open animosity and audacious challenge by Iran to America's might. It is uncertain where U.S. national security stands today in the face of two enemies, Al-Qaeda and Iran, that vow to destroy America's military through an open war of strategic attrition and Islamic Jihad. Nonetheless, the fight against terrorism undeniably achieved some measures of national security for the United States of America, and perhaps the entire world, despite the unpopular war in Iraq and the inability of the West to curb the Islamic expansionism of Iran. President George W. Bush may not have decisively won the entire war in Iraq, but his plan for national security seems to be advancing against all odds due to the effects of the war on the status quo of the Middle East. The present situation in the Middle East may be slowly descending into wider conflicts, as the cold war between the Sunnis and the Shiites continues to engender a situation that might help the U.S. forge future policies in a region relatively more hospitable to American ideas.

The Bush war on terror reshuffled the regional cards in the wider Middle East and began to destabilize a stagnating post-cold war status quo. Israel is beginning to find very obvious Arab sympathizers as the threat of nuclear Iran rises and becomes the number one existential threat to many people in the region. The Palestinian cause has begun to crack from within due to the opposing ideologies of Arab supporters of a "just Palestinian cause for an independent state" and a rejectionist front that includes Hamas, Islamic Jihad, and other anti-peace Palestinian factions, supported by Iran and Syria to destroy the State of Israel. Additionally, state-sponsored terrorism in Syria is widely implicated in the assassination of a number of anti-Syrian figures in Lebanon both before and after the forced withdrawal of Syrian troops from Lebanon. This novel situation in Lebanon has also posed new strategic questions in a country that has been a battleground for ideologies and remains a model for much wider regional conflicts. Additionally, the war in Iraq played best in the hands of the Iranian regime and transformed it into a regional power with increasing leverage in Iraq, Syria, Lebanon, the Palestinian territories and Afghanistan, as well as the struggle between extremist and moderate forces over nuclear Pakistan. Iran leads the anti-America and anti-Israel camp today and stands at the helm of a strategic and popular Shiite Crescent that stretches from Northern Afghanistan, through the Islamic Republic of Iran, Iraq, and Syria, and positions the Mullah regime face-to-face with Israel through Hezbollah in Lebanon. Iran's geo-political and ideological position is by all means the worst American security and strategic nightmare. Iran is skillfully exploiting the current situation in a war of attrition in Iraq, a battle of political hemorrhage in the wider Middle East, and a strategy to engage the U.S. and its European allies over a frightening nuclear question. The conclusion can be straightforward. Either Iran continues to successfully bleed American military capabilities in Iraq and engage the U.S. and its regional and European allies in tense and polarizing diplomacy, or the U.S. handles the situation with more strategic stealth, perhaps by bombing Iran's nuclear facilities. Taken together, the developments in the Middle East and the world post 9/11 may be transforming the Middle East into a zone of proxy wars of a cold war style. Social and cultural trends are not amenable to change through war and a journalistic style of diplomacy, however, the situation in the Middle East is likely to produce good economic, strategic, and military standing for the U.S. should American diplomacy invest in cultural dialogue and policies of strategic long-term partnerships. The traditionally irreconcilable forces in the Middle East are slowly merging, either passively or actively, into subtle allies in the face of terrorist threats and an aggressive Iran aiming to dominate the region and transform it into a platform to destroy "America's superiority." There is an unprecedented opportunity for U.S. and European diplomacy to secure a rather previously inconceivable regional architecture that will ensure the victory of democratic ideals via peace at the expense of war and conflicts. A New Mediterranean with strategically interlocked institutions can provide the ultimate peace solution in the Middle East and can have a direct impact on U.S. and European security. Such a strategy should constitute the necessary platform upon which the United States bases its Mideast policies for many years to come. The changes that followed 9/11 on the world stage in general, and U.S. foreign policy in the Middle East in particular, are paramount and necessitate a concerted regional effort to enable the U.S. to sustain its strategic role and interests in the Middle East. The ubiquitous walk away from war-time stories and sensational diplomacy are measures that U.S. decision makers can adopt to attenuate anti-Americanism and advance education, dialogue, and grass-roots development in the Middle East.

CHAPTER I

Iran's Regional Role and U.S. Policy

Iran's ambition in the Middle East remains to be greatly underappreciated in U.S. Mideast policy. Iran is a very dynamic and proud society, and whether people are supporters or opponents of the Islamic revolution of the Ayatollahs, there is a general belief of entitlement among the Iranians over the Gulf (Persian) region. While political factors are reasons to drive people away from the Mullah regime of the Islamic Republic of Iran, at least publically, the imperialistic drive to have a Persian Empire in the Middle East is a unifying theme for all Iranians. While U.S. policy seems remiss of such fundamental belief in the Iranian way of life, the Western focus is on nuclear proliferation and the inevitable threats that the Islamic Iranian regime poses on the world. Iran's Islamic influence in the Middle East has grown stronger following the American invasion of Iraq, where Iran has found a strategic launching pad to infuse the ideology of its regime into the wider, predominantly Sunni Muslim Middle East. Despite all problems, Muslim Sunnis have been able to hold significant grounds in their open alliance with the United States, including Saudi Arabia and other Gulf States, Egypt, Jordan, and Turkey. The overwhelming Shiite Muslim society of Iran perceives Arab problems as great benefits to its imperialistic ambition to expand the nuclear Persian Empire into the Middle East and come face to face with Europe, and the United States, through an open conflict with Israel and other regional U.S. allies. The Iranian incitement of the Shiite population in Lebanon, Saudi Arabia, Bahrain, Iraq, and Qatar is nothing but a strategic wedge that Iran is attempting to drive among Arab Muslims to win the sympathy and support of the local Shiite population. Iran plans to establish a pan-Shiite front to face American and other Western intervention in the so-called "Muslim affairs." Iran's pro-Shiite and wider regional policy is not altruistically based on the defense of a unifying "Muslim cause," but a blatant attempt to gratify an archetypal conscience in order to re-establish a Persian empire that all Iranians feel they are entitled to have. Iran is well cognizant, and its regime possesses advantageous political dexterity to play on the dilemma of the U.S. and Western relations with an unpredictable Sunni populace that is partly under the influence of Salafi groups such as Al-Qaeda and its world affiliates.

Salafis are primarily Sunnis, but they aim at toppling local Muslim and Arab regimes, and they describe them as supporters and collaborators with the Christian and Jewish infidels. The Salafi ideology is deeply rooted in some factions of Islam all over the globe, particularly in the Middle East and Europe. The ideology calls for an open bloody struggle or Jihad with the West, mainly the U.S. and Europe, as imperialistic powers that robbed the Islamic heritage and established the state systems that currently exist in the Muslim world. According to the Salafi ideology, the state system that is based on Western rules has to be abolished among all Muslims, who have to be unified in Jihad against Western-backed regional regimes, and instead the rule of Shariah has to be installed in a "boundless or border-free Islamic nation." Although Sunni in its interpretation, this ideology finds common ground with the Iranian regime that calls for the "Islamization of the world." The Iranians are staunchly anti-U.S. and perceive the U.S. role in the Middle East as a barrier for their expansion in the region. Moreover, the ideology of the "Islamization of the world" by the Mullah regime of Iran resonates quite well with the Salafis, who find Judaeo-Christian values as the main obstacle for their influence in the world. Therefore, a state of de-facto marriage is currently taking place between the Salafi Sunnis and the Shiite of Iran against the U.S. and its allies; however, both parties seem to be hunting for opportunities to benefit from the demise of the other. The Iranian regime strives to support Al-Qaeda and its loose affiliates in Afghanistan, Pakistan, Southeast Asia, and some Arab states. The Iranian strategy to support Al-Qaeda provides a double-edged sword to weaken both enemies, the U.S. and its allies as well as the Sunni hegemony over Islamic faith and interpretation of the Koran. Iran's ideological approach transcends social, military, and strategic issues to a very deep-rooted psychological and cultural will of revenge for the Sunni slaughter and humiliation of their religious leaders, Imam Ali and Hussein, respectively.

Iran's regional role clashes with U.S. and Western interests at many levels and in many ways. Firstly, the military question and armament of either Israel or Sunni Arab States are inevitably a strategic barrier for Iran to achieve its regional goals. Secondly, the U.S. and Western support to Israel, which is in the eyes of every Muslim an illegitimate implant in the heart of Muslim land and a robbery of Islamic pride, angers Iran at both religious and military levels. Therefore, Iran's support to the Shiite group known as Hezbollah in Lebanon and Sunni groups such as Hamas and Islamic Jihad in the Palestinian territories, as well as the alliance with the Alawite regime in Syria, are part of the Islamic Republic's direct hand in the confrontation with the U.S. and its allies. Thirdly, Iran perceives nuclear armament as a vital element that will impart greater respect, recognition, and fear of the Islamic Republic across the Middle East, Europe, and even the United States. The relentless efforts of the Mullah regime to export the Islamic Revolution and Islamize the world are the nerve of Iran's regional strategy. In the light of Iran's slow but apparently steady development into a nuclear power, the world has been trying in absolute vain to stop the development of an Iranian nuclear bomb. The Iranians only negotiate on the contents of their own ideology in the most classical authoritarian fashion, just to buy time and wait for changes of public opinion and governments in the West to finally forge their ambitions.

The Iranian regime has been able to get away with lots of things without any grave repercussions on its stability and existence. The regime skillfully survived the American hostage crises in the 1980s both in Iran and Lebanon and has been very open about the obvious meddling in the affairs of Lebanon, Iraq, and the Palestinians, in blunt antagonism to the U.S. The lack of decisive American response is taken favorably in Iran and among its regional allies, who think that U.S. actions are based on short-term, unsustainable, and vulnerable policies that, beyond the protection of Israel and the oil reserves of Saudi Arabia, have not served U.S. allies in the region. The Iranians point the fingers at flaws in past U.S. alliances with Saddam Hussein during the 1980's Iraq-Iran war and Bin Laden in Afghanistan as examples of U.S. vulnerability. Iran backs Hezbollah in Lebanon militarily, financially, and ideologically as their closest and most important ally in the region, because this Shiite group provides a direct front with Israel in South Lebanon. The Hezbollah anti-U.S. platform has never been punished; Imad Mughnieh, a top intelligence and military leader of Hezbollah, was assassinated in Syria in February 2008 and was implicated in a number of attacks on U.S. interests, including the bombing of the U.S. Embassy and U.S. Marines in Beirut, and a number of terrorist attacks, for which Hezbollah got a slap on the wrist by the U.S. State Department adding it as a terrorist group on the list of terrorist organizations. Hezbollah and Palestinian groups, such as Hamas and Islamic Jihad, receive strong support from Iran and Syria for their attacks on Israel and their opposition of the Mideast peace process. Iran also supports the Shiites of Iraq, with whom the U.S. government formed an open alliance to topple the regime of Saddam Hussein. These elements render Iranian propaganda among Muslims in the Middle East and beyond more convincing than non-persistent American policies. For example, Hezbollah, Syria, Iran, and Palestinian groups in Lebanon consistently point the fingers at America's abandonment of its allies in Lebanon following the bombing of U.S. Marines. This incident gives America's enemies in the Middle East a sense of empowerment largely based on beliefs that the U.S. public opinion will turn around as soon as they display the slightest resistance to America's will in the region. Unfortunately, the American public often falls in the trap of its own enemy when they rush to change policies and strategies rather than face the issues with resilience and determination. Iran's regime made it clear several times that the Shiite resistance, Al-Qaeda, and the Iraqi insurgents will soon manage to wear the American patience very thin and that will lead to the exit of U.S. troops from Iraq so Iran can fill the vacuum left after the collapse of the Sunni regime. It appears that the only way for the U.S. and its allies to face Iranian expansionism in the Middle East is to empower and support local allies who have both strategic and existential interests to do the fight for the U.S. This strategy will also provide the U.S. with a strategic buffer against changes of American public opinion, which greatly influence the endurance and persistence of U.S. foreign policy. At the same time, the U.S. can work with the local governments and populations toward a universal development at all levels so the people of the Middle East recognize the fact that human prosperity depends on the will of people to develop it and defend it. The U.S. ought to hybridize its own interests with those of its regional allies to generate more security as well as successful and viable long-term policies.

Chapter II

Sunni and Shiite Muslims: A Never Ending Schism

Since the rise of Islam around 460 C.E. the struggle between Sunni and Shiite Muslims has not stopped. Sunni means "law" in Arabic and it refers to the original laws of Islam. Muslim Sunnis claim that their teachings stem directly from the Prophet Mohammed's words through the Koran and Hadith. Hadith, or "speech," refers to the personal speeches of the Prophet Mohammed. Following the death of the Prophet Mohammed, a bitter struggle erupted between his closest lieutenants, including Ali Ben Abi Taleb who is the closest in kin to the Prophet, and a succession of Caliphates (rulers), including Mouaweah. Prior to his death, the Prophet was asked who should inherit his heir as the head of the new Islamic faith. The Prophet answered that the person who is closest to him should inherit the heir. During the conversation, Mouaweah, one of the most known Sunni Caliphates, was sitting near the prophet, so Mouaweah and his followers interpreted the Prophet's response that he should be the Prophet's successor, or next Caliphate. However, Ali and his followers interpreted the Prophet's response that the closest in kin, meaning Ali who was related to the Prophet, should be the successor. Since then a bloody feud erupted between Sunnis and Shiites. Shiite means "allegiance," or loyalty to Ali as the Prophet's closest relative. The Shiites remained Ali's staunchest followers until they were split between Shiites and Alawites, in reference to Ali, following an infamous incident known as "Al-Tahkim," or contest, in which Shiites claimed that the Caliphate tricked Ali, taking advantage of his honesty and word of honor. The Alawites protested Ali's acceptance of the results of the contest and called on him to denounce it, and they defected, whereas the Shiites maintained allegiance to Ali. The competition between the Sunnis on one hand and Shiites and Alawites on the other hand resulted in the battle of

Karballa of Iraq, which led to the Shiites' loss of the war and the dominion of the Sunnis. The Shiite bitterness not only stems from the loss of the Caliphate to the Sunnis but also to the alleged killing of Imam Ali's son Hussein by the Sunnis at the battle of Karballa.

The struggle between Sunni and Shiite Muslims is almost of an archetypal nature. The Sunnis became the most dominant Muslim faction in the Middle East and among non-Arab Muslims, who today constitute the overwhelming majority of Sunni Muslims. Sunnis include the majority of Muslims in Afghanistan, Pakistan, India, China, Indonesia (the world's largest Muslim nation), and Malaysia, African and Asian countries, the Middle East, and the Arab world. The Shiites became a minority and regressed into various regions of Iraq, and then they spread into Iran, which is today's largest Shiite nation, and other parts of the Persian Gulf, including Bahrain, Qatar, and certain parts of Afghanistan, Saudi Arabia, and Lebanon. The Alawites remained in Syria, where they constitute around 10 percent of the overwhelming Sunni population. The Alawites are the closest to the Shiites, and they seized power in Syria in the late 1960s to become the country's most politically dominant group, maintaining a Stalinist regime under the banner of the Baath party of Syria. The Baath party is a Stalinist one-party system that calls for Greater Syria, which includes Syria, Iraq, Israel, Lebanon, and the Palestinian territories. The Baath regime of Syria is not supposed to be a factional or sectarian group, according to the Baath Charter, but the aim of Greater Syria and the Alawites' domination of the Syrian political process bring the regime very close with the Shiites of Iran and Lebanon. Iran's aim to have a direct front with Israel and the ideological and political allegiance of the Lebanese Shiites to Iran rendered the Syrian Alawite regime a strategic asset for Iran's expansion into the Middle East. The Baathist ideology and the role of Alawites in Syrian politics meet fertile grounds in Iran, where the Shiites perceive the Alawites as their historical allies and closest Muslims against Sunni dominion. Secularism proved to be effective in the hands of the minority Alawite regime of Syria to oppress the majority Sunni voice and helped the Baath regime maintain its tight grip on Syria's decision making process. Sunni uprisings in Syria have been long awaited, and several attempts by the Muslim Brotherhood groups were brutally crushed by the existing regime.

Nonetheless, Syria's regime finds vital strategic and existential interests with the Shiite Mullah regime of

Iran. Following the fall of Saddam Hussein and the rise of Iraqi Shiites, a new strategic entity, known as the "Shiite Arch," has stretched from Iran through Iraq via the Syrian Alawites to Lebanon's Shiite community. The strategic arch has not only provided the Shiites with a new breath to challenge the U.S. and the Sunnis but also created an unprecedented direct front for Muslim Shiites with Israel. This front is Iran's most valuable strategic victory in the region, where it can use Hezbollah in Lebanon to press Israel. Iran has indeed brought about Hezbollah with Syria's complacency and directly contributed to the hostage crisis of the 1980s in order to press the U.S. and its Western allies to change their pro-Israel policy in the Middle East. Hezbollah is a Shiite organization that was mainly established in Iran and helped install the Mullah regime of the Islamic Republic. Iran's Imam Khomeini ideology to Islamize the world and establish a Mullah-style theocratic state infiltrated the Lebanese Shiites. The Iranian Revolutionary Guards trained, armed, and sponsored Hezbollah, and masterminded the bombing of U.S. Marines in Beirut, which led to the killing of around 250 soldiers and contracting Lebanon to Syria. Hezbollah still adopts a charter to establish an Iranian-style Islamic state in Lebanon and aims to "liberate

Jerusalem from the Zionists," and destroy the State of Israel. Hezbollah serves a great favor to the Syrian regime, which not only finds Hezbollah as a common strategic asset with Iran, but also helps Syria use Hezbollah as a card on the negotiation table with the U.S., Israel, and the West. The Alawites' bargaining chip has recently expanded from Lebanon into Iraq, where Iranian-influenced Shiites such as the Mahdi Army of Mugtada Al Sader, are battling against both the U.S. and Iraqi Sunnis with Iranian-Syrian support. The numerous fronts that Iran and Syria have created as proxy wars against the U.S. and its allies in Lebanon, Iraq, and the Palestinian territories, where both countries openly support the opponents of the peace process, are giving the theocratic regime in Iran more time and assets to achieve its aims in the Middle East and the world. The rise of the Shiites in Iraq and Lebanon along the ideology of the Iranian regime should alarm the U.S. and its allies, including Europe, Israel, and most Arab states. It is a unique time when the interests of most Sunni Arabs intersect with the interests of Israel, including Fatah in the Palestinian territories, where Iranian and Syrian influence has managed to detach Hamas from the Muslim Sunni world. Hamas and Islamic Jihad receive their support from

Iran today following an Iranian backed separatist move by the hardliners in the Gaza strip. Iran is interested in delaying every conflict in the region in order to gain time to develop its nuclear and ballistic arsenal. The Coup D'etat that Hamas led against Fatah in Gaza is nothing but a single step in Iran's milestone for a Shiite architecture in the Middle East. The U.S. and its allies are faced with a real enemy that has strong grassroots support this time. This enemy is not the Soviet Union or Nazi Germany; this is an ideologically driven force that conceives its policies from past experiences and designs its strategies towards a theocratically appealing style of social welfare, religious brain-washing, and demographic distribution that has only proved to widen and spread.

Israel might have tried to capitalize on unsuccessful alliances with minorities in the Middle East and aspired to work with, perhaps, a secular Iran to conquer Arab rejection of its existence. However, Israel's strategy today is facing challenges from the groups whom the Jewish State may have historically perceived as potential allies, the Shiites. The Shiite world, except the Gulf state of Qatar that has full diplomatic relations with Israel, is currently totally anti-Israel, as its existence and power will provide all justifications to prevent the making of nuclear Iran. Nuclear Iran is the Sunni Arabs' worst nightmare and a painful reality that Europe and possibly Russia have to exist with. It is a valuable time in history when old foes are aligned in the face of fear of nuclear proliferation and destruction. Besides the nuclear question, Islamic extremists among the Sunnis are promising a return to the era of the Caliphates and the destruction of all national, religious, and human boundaries that dismember the Islamic nation. This kind of ideology has a perfect echo within the Iranian regime since the enemies of Iran's enemy are the Mullahs' friends. Despite the factional divide between Shiite Iran and Sunni extremists, including Hamas in the Palestinian territories and the Salafi ideology of Al-Qaeda, Iran continues to support the causes of these groups. The overlapping goals of Salafi Jihadists and Hamas include the destruction of the State of Israel and hence rejection of any peace negotiation between the Palestinians and Israel. Both Iran and Salafis aim to overturn pro-American Arab regimes and weaken U.S. military, economic, and strategic presence in the world. Once again, the interests of many old enemies are now reshuffled to make the cards of a new strategic alliance. Russia, the U.S., Europe, moderate Arab states, and the entire world have borne the brunt of terrorism in the last few years. Israel, along with U.S.-supported Arab regimes, the U.S., and Europe have been battling a common enemy, which is strategically united with Iran. The wedge that the Iraq war has driven between Sunni and Shiite Arabs is expected to widen the gap between Iran and its allies (Shiites, Alawites and Sunni Salafis) on one hand and moderate Sunnis, the U.S., and Israel on the other hand. This reality is already manifest in the Palestinian-Israeli context, which is the mother of all issues in the Middle East, where Israel and the Palestinian authority are in de-facto alliance against Iran-supported Hamas despite the deep-rooted mistrust between the two sides. The isolation of Hamas and the sharp decrease of Arab support for Hezbollah as well as the active Arab backing of Iraqi Sunnis against the Shiites, Iran, and Al-Qaeda are clear indications that the current polarization of the region necessitates a historic peace among the "subtle" allies. Taken together, these issues inevitably provide novel strategies for an ultimate peace solution in the Middle East. The world is witnessing positive polarization between the forces of moderation and ethno-religious coexistence and the delinquency of ideological destruction of both peace and life.

CHAPTER III

Culture and Democracy

The exigencies of peaceful solutions to the existing clash between hardline extremists and the desirable existential harmony between moderate forces require cultural understanding. The corruption of ideas and destruction of values will not help bring about peace or annihilate the dangers of terrorism and extremism. Western cultures are grounded in Judaeo-Christian values from which respect for human rights and the human being largely evolved. That respect strengthened the notion of democracy in Western political systems and promoted freedom of expression. The practice of democracy in the West did not translate into universal practices nor witness the application of democracy and human rights in the world context. Western powers, especially Europeans, colonized many regions of the world, where they were perceived as oppressors and thieves of local resources and identities. The West transformed the invaluable concepts of democracy, human rights, and prosperity at home into tools of dominion. Democracy and human rights evolved out of centuries of human suffering in the West and they would only flourish in the same way in other civilizations.

On the other side of the spectrum, Islam struggles with the concept of Western modernity. Islam remains strictly attached to the teachings of the Koran, which do not separate religion from the state. In Western societies, separation between religion and the state is very highly desirable, whereas in Islamic societies, politics and governance have to stem largely from religion. This is a fundamental political and cultural difference between the West and Islam. In Islam, no matter how liberal the system is set to be, religion will still dominate the scene of political behavior. Issues that range from elections, to finance and loans, to the rights of other faiths to exist besides Islam, are dilemmas that Islamic societies attempt to evade. Since religion encodes societal and cultural values, Islamic cultural trends are fatal to a democratic Western system. The idea that people should lift sufferings in Islamic teaching is undermined by suspicion that global economic, political, and strategic relations hinder such popular progress. As such, the human rights of the individual in Islamic societies are tightly linked to the so-called rights of Muslims in the world. In Western societies, where Islam is growing and gaining ground, governmental systems do not discriminate between Muslims and non-Muslims, but treat all citizens as equal before the law. Muslims on the other hand not only take the individual human rights and dignity for granted, but they also try to gain collective religious rights at the expense of the human rights of the individual. Christians, Jews, Buddhists, etc., do not have problems practicing their religious beliefs in Western societies, but Muslims do have significant problems, perceiving the system as a culture that works against them. The integration of Islamic communities into Western culture has proven to be a timed bomb that will explode any time, whereas the integration of non-Muslims in Islamic societies is a forgotten issue. The cultural fate of non-Muslim groups in Islamic societies is in a progressive demise since massive migration is observed from Muslim countries in fear of oppression and extremism. Non-Muslims are forced out of their lands and stripped of their cultures in the majority of Muslim countries, where Islamization of culture and way of life, besides political persecution, have been taking place. In many countries of the Middle East, Christian groups are facing pressure not from the extremists, but from ordinary Muslim co-patriots, to leave their own land and avoid life as second-class citizens. Muslims in the West, on the other hand, are not subjected to this kind of existential pressure. Islam and Muslim communities continue to grow and press for more social and religious rights in Europe, the United States, Australia, and other places. Islam seems to be taking advantage of democracy in order to expand and grow in the West, but not to reform political and social practices in Islamic societies.

The clash of civilizations is true so far as one group fails to understand and respect the values of another group. Strict religious practices in Islam blind so many Muslims from seeing that life is "fun" in the eyes of Westerners. Western cultures have the concept of "fun" at the core of their understanding of life, which includes economic prosperity, political stability through people's power to change their government, drinking and clubbing, seizing important opportunities, etc. Westerners fail to appreciate that the Muslims' understanding of life is largely based on religious beliefs and practices, which constitute the path to eternal happiness and the other life. The concept of an eternal life is also true for other monolithic religions, but while Judaeo-Christian traditions have adapted to civil and social norms, Islam is still intolerant in that regard. That clash emanates largely from moral deception and corruption within the cultures. The problem in the West is predominantly racism as religion has been on the decline over the last century, especially in Europe. Although the West is predominantly Christian in origin and tradition, a third generation African American, whether Christian or not, is still perceived as an African American, while a third generation German or Norwegian becomes 100 percent American as long as he or she loses the accent and blends with the Caucasian population. So in the West, the physical appearance and racial origin diminish belonging to the culture not only because people maintain their original ethnic culture, but also because of color and the perception of a broadly "white" Western society. There is undeniably an unconscious inclination in that "Western is white," due to the fact that Western civilization took place in continental Europe. As much as Western Christiandom and the notions of free societies are amenable to racial slurring, profiling, and subordination, so is Islam in determining the infidels and judging other religions. For example, the majority of Muslim Arabs see a Christian Arab, who is indigenous in the Middle East and is loyal to his Arab culture, language, and traditions, as marginal, irrelevant, and sometimes an intruder into the Islamic way of life. When minority Christian groups migrate from their motherlands mostly to the West, intending to be loyal and to faithfully adopt a new way of life, they are subjected to cultural and ethnic subordination. Despite the fact that a Middle Eastern Christian perceives himself as similar in his Christian traditions to the West, he still falls victim of perceptions both in his motherland and the country of adoption. Additionally, descendents of Western societies have stigmatized many indigenous people, including aboriginal Australians, American Indians, Maoris, etc, and set themselves to be the custodians and the owners of the "new land," masters of new culture, and the pioneers of society.

Islam is not much more welcoming of cultural diversity, despite the fact that there are Muslim Arabs,

Asians, Europeans, etc. No matter what the racial denomination or proportion of world Muslims are, Arabs still feel that they are the custodians of Islam. Intolerance in Islam is mostly, but not exclusively, manifest in the rejection of the extremists to other religions. The twenty-first century witnessed strong evidence of that effect. The persecution of Muslims in the Balkan at the hands of Christians created an overwhelming sympathy among the world Muslim population. However, the persecution of Christians in the Middle East, and particularly the Arab world, has not awakened Christianity in the West to salvage Christiandom in that part of the world. The rights of white Zimbabwean farmers (14,000) mobilized the European continent against the Mugabe regime, which set the standards to strip white farmers of their powers and wealth in order to redistribute them to the local African population. The rise of Islam in favor of European Muslims was to salvage Islam and ensure that it spreads deeper into Europe, while the reaction of the West to the Mugabe fiasco was to protect the white minority, in stark contrast to Western indifference to protect Christian minorities in the Middle East. The West has to pose an inevitable question as to why minorities are facing existential annihilation in the

Muslim world, whereas Islam seems to prosper and spread in Western societies. A double-edged challenge has to be considered, including the extent to which Islam can exist with other religions, especially in Islamic societies, and the willingness of the West to clearly distinguish between tolerance of the Islamic religion and the inability to deal with the invasion of Western civilization by Islamism. The Western mind only began to react in religious terms on mass scales following the 9/11 terrorist attacks on the World Trade Center in New York City and the Pentagon. Cultural mix, migration, and the information age have contributed greatly to the hybridization of cultures and introduced interlocking values to the core of world civilizations. However, the right of custodianship and the feeling of "originality" in each culture create rigidity in values and conspicuity in the presentation of cultural trends. Originality is a claim that engenders frustration and leads to mass alienation in an increasingly cosmopolitan world. Cultural corruption based on racial preferences, religious intolerance, or social unacceptance are invariably similar in their effects. For the elimination of the so-called clash of civilizations, each group ought to understand its place in history and relevance to the future and respect the differential evolution of others. The ultimate clash of civilizations entails an attempt to maintain the concept of "originality" and persistence to have the exclusive right of one group to determine what is right and wrong for others.

Chapter IV

September 11, 2001, and the Defeated Purpose

The events that followed the tragedies of 9/11 delineated new territories on the world stage and opened up the way for more racial profiling. This dilemma exacerbated the clash of civilizations along with the sweeping victories of right wing politicians to executive government in Italy, Spain, Australia, the U.S., and other countries. The change in the public mood seemed to encourage policy makers, particularly in the United States of America, to tighten the grip on certain ethno-religious groups, particularly Muslims. Radical steps were taken to control terrorism, which led to obvious racial profiling, primarily at points of entry into the country, besides the role played by the media. The usual counterbalance of the views of right wing politicians and neo-conservatives by the traditional left wing camp of activists and politicians was very timid, to say the least. There definitely appeared to be an overwhelming righteous fear of the spread of Islamism in the world. The numerous terrorist attacks in various parts of the world including Europe, the Middle East, and Southeast Asia unraveled an unprecedented threat to the values and way of life of the free world. Taken together, the events that followed the terrorist attacks of 9/11 drove Islamic fear even deeper, and the invasion of Iraq greatly shook the psyche of the Islamic civilization and led to collective emotional and political resistance to every attempt to equate terror with Islam. Furthermore, 9/11 not only showed the vulnerability of the free world in the face of dangerous backward Islamic ideologies but also exposed the extent of ignorance among and between the West and Islam. Islamic terrorism is a manifestation of both religious frustration and Western alienation in the eyes of the terrorists. Besides the constant brainwashing of Islamists and calls for Jihad, there is a reinforcement of the culture of animosity between Islam and the West. Islam regards Western powers as the main obstacle towards its expansion and Islamization of the world and considers the abortion of advancement in Islamic countries as a conspiracy to maintain Western hegemony of the world. Islam does not consider religious teachings and governmental policies as reasons for lack of economic, democratic, and social advancement in the Muslim world, but lays the blame squarely on foreign intervention and conspiratorial designs for the Islamic world. Therefore, cultural, religious, and economic factors collectively contribute to engender terrorism. On the other side of the political spectrum, mobilization of public opinion based on the extent of the tragedies that followed the terror attacks in the U.S. and the world is a failed policy and a state of mortal strategic hemorrhage that no country, or even superpower, can sustain. The Western world, including the U.S. and Europe, still seem confused between their desire to coexist with Islam as a "peaceful" religion, and the growing tendencies to stop its spread and fight the people who propagate it as a state model and way of life. This is a difficult situation where democratic values have to prevail to accept others, and there exists the need to protect democracy from its worst enemies, including terrorism and religious fundamentalism. The ultimate goal of governments and their authorities is to stop terrorism and protect their citizens and the image of their administrations. This goal can only be achieved by understanding the cultural codes, which primarily include religion, in the countries that oppose our policies and the groups that resort to terrorism to defeat us. This objective seems to have been defeated on many fronts and in many different ways. Even though terrorists are under increasingly more scrutiny by government and public measures, they continue to instill more fear and intimidation among the average people, thus counteracting the effects of government policies.

The main objective of 9/11 and other terrorist attacks is to instill fear that can kill Western values from within. The lack of personal and national security is at the helm of the terrorists' strategy to tell Western democracies and their allies that no one is invincible. Destructive fear is meant to paralyze cities, economies, flow of people and ideas, and the spread of Western values. Terror is meant to create suspicion that would have a direct impact on world economy and security by raising doubts about the willingness of Western democracies to accept Muslims as equal partners on the world stage. The reaction of Western societies to terrorism can only defeat the purpose of the terrorists if balance and caution are exercised. It should be remembered that the overwhelming majority of people on earth lack necessary and basic education. The average person should be a primary target for education so terrorists do not penetrate their way of life by cultivating ignorance and hatred of the West. For example, when the torture prisons of Saddam Hussein became those of the coalition forces, more paranoia and less certainty were the dominant factors among the average people. The idea of a free society based on democratic principles and ideals cannot be disseminated by force and invasion. Mounting popular paranoia, dwindling certainty, growing economic hardships, and weakened global security are now a common denominator among all people. The terrorists may certainly not have won the hearts and minds of people, but they shook their belief systems, and that can potentially provide "excellent" tools to alienate the public from the truth in the guise of safety and security. Nothing was learned from terrorism if the increased awareness of evil is accompanied by increasingly diabolic rigidity. Political and cultural rigidity only lead to mounting frustration, so those on the Western side lose touch with reality and the truth, and those on the vulnerable side of being swayed and influenced by the terrorists become more readily absorbed by religious slogans and extremism.

Intellects in our societies are not necessarily those who own the microphone and get to theorize about the world. Our societies are in dire need for the power of the intellect to influence our thinking and way of life. Worldly intellects are capable of bridging the cultural gaps that exist between the civilizations, beginning with the daily practice that ranges from collective social boredom to the individualistic life. Certain societies where economic prosperity and political stability are lacking suffer greatly from a state of collective social boredom, so religion plays a fundamental role in shaping people's minds. Religion replaces the role that an intellect plays in identifying the relevance of history and existence to present and future events. The absence of intellects prevent cultural renaissance, and thus political reform, in societies where religious teaching has replaced the indispensability of new ideas. On the contrary to religiously influenced societies, the power of communications and particularly the media in fast-pace Western societies is not only hijacking the impact of intellectualism but also undermining valuable human-to-human interaction. Social boredom and life influenced by mental shortcuts and selective quick media reports further necessitate the creation of world systems that counteract this clash of civilizations. Peace can only be brought about when it becomes an individual's state of mind and a collective way of life, so the need is there to delineate a strategy that lays the foundation for peace. Cultural diversity gains its significance from the historical experience of people and the binding values that bring coalescence among the different races, and there is a lot of commonality among societies to reconcile their cultural and religious differences. Unless both Islam and the West learn from the 9/11 experience to mold their strategic approaches and reshape their mutual cultural views, no one would have improved on the unfortunate consequences of the one of the world's most memorable strategic and human catastrophes.

Chapter V

The Corruption of Ideas

The disharmony that splits cultures apart exists in the corruption of the idea of "originality." The concept of originality shapes cultural practices and is paramount in causing rigidity, so every culture claims custodianship of certain values and calls on successive generations to adhere to them. Ownership and custodianship of traditions render cultural practices unamenable to change, which may prevent generational harmony and peace. Even though religion and language encode some of the fundamental principles of culture, it is problematic to equate culture with religion, i.e. Arabism and Islam and Christianity and the

West. These concepts of cultural rigidity become very difficult to penetrate by educational means, which guarantee openness and cultural flexibility. At the helm of the clash of civilizations lies not only fundamentalism but also corruption of ideas that even in a supposedly secular or modern society, the claim of originality underlies "perceived" cultural and religious superiority. The claim that certain cultures have invented democracy and social justice while others have to learn is a source of endless conflict. Cultural evolution is a process that took many centuries to unfold and advance towards democracy, however, religion seems to have slowed this progression, especially in the Islamic faith, where the rights of non-Muslims are granted as second-class citizens. Western cultures assert that they are the inventors of democracy, which has evolved out of the West, but Muslims claim to be the givers of human rights according to the Koran. Democracy could not have been a value that emanated from Western societies unless its roots were deeply buried in pre-existing societies, so the idea of democracy is not exclusively Western. The West adopts the concept of democracy and propagates it as a Western value in line with cultural and societal traditions, and Islam reacts to it as Western rather than a human value. Islam, on the other hand, claims to be a pioneer in establishing laws of social justice to all Muslims. However, unlike Western belief in democracy, which should prevail for the good of all people, Islam considers social justice a doctrine only through Islam. It is arguable whether any culture has an exclusive right to claim the establishment of a human value. Therefore, even though the practice of values varies across ethno-religious groups, the claim of originality is likely to corrupt the concepts and lead to their annihilation through conflicts and competition.

Freedom of expression is the right of every individual and a responsibility for everyone to carry. Prior and in the aftermath of the U.S.-led coalition war in Iraq, millions of demonstrators took down to the streets of New York City and London protesting the war, and this was described as a vivid manifestation of democracy. However, when the same demonstrations took place in Cairo, Paris, or other countries opposed to the war, they were interpreted as anti-Americanism or support to the brutality of Saddam Hussein's regime. How does the freedom of expression differ within and between cultures? Corrupting a concept is making it relevant to particular times and circumstances, while denying it to others under different or similar circumstances. For example, Beirut was portrayed as a terrorist city when terrorists bombed the multi-national peacekeeping forces, including French and American troops, during the country's civil war (1975-1990), whereas when terrorists attacked New York City for the same purpose they attacked Westerners in Beirut in the mid 1980s, the two events did not receive the same interpretation. In both instances, terrorists of very similar political and religious beliefs, which include among other things the destruction of America's influence in the Middle East, attacked various U.S. interests in order to force the incumbent U.S. Administration to change its policies vis-à-vis Israel. The attacks on New York City were rightly described a terrorist aggression against the U.S., while the attacks in Beirut were portrayed as those of a terrorist city on Westerners. The list is endless. Since cultural trends are partly based on perception, an interpretation of an event can shape the wider public opinion and create cultural perception of a particular place, people, and time.

Tarnishing the reputation of places is one form of corruption of ideas that leads to prevention of positive human relations. For example, the lack of democratic institutions is undeniably a cultural deficit in the modern day societies of Iraq and Iran; both the perpetrators of the existing status quo in those countries and their opponents or enemies jointly corrupt the significance of time in that part of the world. By time I mean the impact of history on the day-to-day functioning of the people. While these societies are largely complacent that they have played a considerable role in history through civilizations that existed and prospered for centuries, they still view their pride as an integral part of that success. In fact, the corruption of cultural ideals with such an unjustified complacency with the past is driving societies backward as if their ancestors have done the jobs for them. Some Westerners view the existing situation in Iran and Iraq as barbaric based on digital media reports that describe the place at its present moment. The perception of barbarism is solely based on periods of lawlessness and anarchy due to the absence of democratization, and it is as dangerous as cultural complacency because it discounts the importance of the human to lay the foundations of modern societies. The golden ages of local empires, including the Persian, Babylonian, Assyrian, etc., laid the fundamentals of science, trade, the state system, and industry, which contributed greatly to

Western success and civilization. Societies ought to understand the extent to which they have inherited from one another throughout time and that neither race nor geography contribute to either failure or success, rather it is the human will to accept and build on the achievements of others for the universal benefits of humanity.

Societal thoughts can also be corrupted when every group thinks they are right. Americans live in little technology boxes and they often mesmerize on a frightening pleasure of national superiority. Criticism of the American way by others is a mortal sin, as is the case in most developed countries, where technological advances, fledgling democracies, and elevated living standards gratify an inner feeling that success in many aspects of life implies cultural infallibility. Other societies also perceive their cultural invincibility from other perspectives, often based on historical significance and success. Islamic societies strive to create a perception that the Islamic way of life, including social, spiritual, and existential characters, is by far the best, and Muslims have a duty to Islamize the world to make it a better place. Unfortunately, certain societies misunderstand and confuse the legitimacy of competition with the creation of a mood of combativeness.

The need to better someone's life is largely based on the individual's benefit from historical achievements and advances, so present day success should not be mistaken for superiority and, most importantly, racial success. Societies have evolved in different ways depending on their geo-political, religious, and demographic distribution, and unless evolution is respected, societies will remain in the illusion of superiority.

A short attention span is a dominant factor in American society, and it is an epidemic of immense social ramifications. The televisionation of crime, science, the economy, and every aspect of life gives a fair impression that things get done quickly and without laborious work. The relative abundance of wealth and material means transformed the American society into a superficial entity, which is heavily reliant on pragmatism and short cuts. This American trend is globalized with the help of the media and is becoming a universal tendency. In the light of all that we observe, and despite the proportionally high government spending on science and research, everybody likes to see things done like a television advertisement, while the emphasis on the deeper meaning of life is fading from the human psyche. Individualism adds to social isolation among an increasingly greater number of people and makes the television and all it encompasses with quick fixes and sensationalism the frontier for people's learning and experiences. A frightening tendency exists among lots of Americans to judge national groups according to aberrant and ill-researched television shows. For example, implicating the entire Arabic culture in terrorism solely based on the events of 9/11 is not only a perceptual but also a cultural mistake that an entire nation is likely to make due to dissemination of false sensational information that make an ill-informed media the major educator of the nation. Based on the speed of execution of televised information, people have learned to understand that most things might happen in a rather simplistic way. A spoilt population cannot appreciate the sufferings of others, thus eliminating cultural compatibility. The media has definitely reduced the time people spend on reading in comparison to watching television or surfing often unacademic sites of the Internet. Media reports have also managed to construct an image of a self-centered society, where every citizen thinks that everybody hates Americans, while other cultures and societies may also think that America's might is out there to get them. However, it should not be forgotten that societal struggle to prove righteousness is eventually a relative phenomenon.

Short cuts to everything and quick fixes to problems undermine human patience, so lack of perseverance becomes unavoidable. The absence of the human will to relate to others leads to the decline of informed conversations and constitutes a frightening epidemic in today's societies. Societal loneliness produces a collective culture of selfishness and exclusivism, while ignorance and lack of education make people victims of perceptions and stereotypes. For examples, a terrorist's nationality should not lead to suspicion of an entire nation, because no culture is a safe heaven for terrorism. Some analysts and experts on terrorism tend to be very shallow and very culturally oriented rather than educational. Exchange of knowledge and information and the promotion of education between cultures create an environment of openness and facilitate an outreach approach that is likely to attenuate disparity between people. In this context, it is imperative to mention that education and exchange of information should not blind people of the essence of their existence relative to the other. For example, the quest for Islamism in Europe is quite different from the U.S. If Europe continues at the same pace of Islamic growth without cultural dialogue and understanding between Islam and the local cultures, Europe will be on the way to a continental Lebanonization. Islam is growing in Europe both in number and influence, and what goes on in the traditional continent seems to take only time to spread to America. The European communities are very preoccupied with economic growth and rationalization, while an ever-growing sympathetic force for Islam continues to shake the security of the continent. The fate of Europe with the Islamic faith is strongly influenced by the geographical proximity to the Middle East and the spread of Islam at all European fronts with an Islamic eagerness and struggle for domination. Europe is a prototype of future America, where Islamism and cultural incompatibility are so strong and can only be reconciled by education at the grassroots level. Therefore, the corruption of ideas can change the significance of time, tarnish the reputation of societies, and create precedence for conflicts. The clash of civilization is partly a process of corruption of societal ideals, through which people claim exclusivism and superiority.

CHAPTER VI

Democracy and Corporate Journalism

Modern diplomacy seems to be deeply misguided on the issue of advancement and promotion of democracy. While world democracies certainly share a responsibility to facilitate economic developments and cultural exchange with non-democratic nations, diplomacy is often mixed with forceful decisions to curb opposition to policies advocated by powerful democracies. In addition to the use of force and international organizations such as the United Nations, World Bank, and other non-government entities, powerful democracies adopt policies that often do not lead to promotion of democracy. Broad-based education among the people of non-democratic nations is the most effective stimulus to conceive of and establish democratic institutions. Democracy is an evolutionary processes and not a revolutionary human endeavor, and therefore, education and not diplomatic negotiations can guaranty its progression. One of the most striking examples of our time was the effort of the U.S. Bush-Cheney administration to promote democracy in Iraq. Ironically, this attempt to engender democracy not only claimed thousands of American and Iraqi lives but also led to civil war that threatened to take its toll on the entire region. The archetypal memories, which widen the schism between Sunni and Shiite Muslims in Iraq and the Islamic world, make democracy more complicated than any government could diplomatically handle. History cannot be plastered over, and so democracy cannot flourish and yield fruitful solutions until the social grounds are ready and ripe. No diplomacy can ignore the historical quarrels between the two great factions of Islam, and therefore, education about Islam, primarily among western journalists and diplomats, is an absolute requirement. In addition to diplomacy that attempts to simplify the issues and force democracy on unfavorable grounds, the media does not help to achieve a diplomatically impossible mission. For example, in Iraq the media seemed to add to the bitterness of alienation and forges a sentiment of superiority by an occupying force against an occupied people. Corporate journalism, which relies heavily on well-defined and pre-planned topics, ignores a great deal of the sensitivities of the local population, further complicating the diplomatic mission to establish democracy amid chaos. Unfortunately corporate journalism trails behind politics and is so often skewed for obvious political objectives. Are we supposed to believe that the smart journalism of the twenty-first century, which was so benevolent in support of the U.S. invasion of Iraq in 2003, was not cognizant of the political deception that was very obviously propagated by the "diplomacy" of the Bush Administration? If we were to assume that the Iraq issue presented a conundrum to the media, whereby the truth could have passed some journalists, we are remiss of our duties as intelligent citizens to forgo the fact that the media still ignored the voice of the people opposing the war, and they probably were the majority. The international pressure on the U.S. Administration not to resort to force to topple Saddam Hussein's regime was bluntly ignored by corporate journalism, which rallied behind the Administration in defiance of public opinion. It is frightening to see the extent to which corporate media trail behind politics. The U.S. government's rhetoric to continue the Iraq war effort by accusing the opponents of the war of failing their patriotic duties to support the troops clearly became the most sensational headline for U.S. media. It suffices to say that the reasons why the Administration dragged the troops to the war were obviously to control oil production in Iraq and the Gulf region. It seems that the link between the rise in oil prices to an unprecedented high of over one hundred dollars a barrel and the war has again escaped the corporate media. This is an issue of worldwide importance, where the media no more makes politics as much as politics defines the media. Interviewing CEOs of major oil companies has been used as a strategy of deflection and management of public anger at the pump and the rising cost of living. If the media is cognizant of all these facts, then its willingness to withhold the truth from the public turns the power of the word into a culture of public deception. In this culture of public deception by corporate journalism, freedom of speech seems to depend on who owns the microphone. The powerful always own the stage to talk, and the backing of a corporate media to an uneducated diplomacy is a fatal attempt to establish democracy. The belligerence of the media and its inability to dissociate itself from imprudent government policies is playing well in the hands of the enemies of democracy, namely Islamic terrorism. The grass-root is able to distinguish between a foreign war and the establishment of democracy, therefore, the uncritical support of corporate media at the early stages of the Iraq war, leads to reinforcement of the premises of terrorism to fight and destroy the enemies of Islam.

Political pragmatism must not determine the boundaries of journalism. The media obviously complies with politicians who convince the public that certain dictatorships, which owns nuclear weapons in a volatile Islamic society, are friendly with the U.S. This call by the media to differentiate between friendly and non-friendly dictatorships is nothing but management of public perception that diplomacy attempts to establish. No dictatorship should be treated more favorably than another if the binding principle of a free society is democracy and freedom for all. Corporate journalism tries, as an outside analytical power, to give a false assessment of the extent of suffering under dictatorships. Freedom is indivisible and uncompromisable and any attempt to assume that the total lack of democracy, or part thereof, is subject to our judgment is an act of arrogance. In summary, corporate journalism is failing to set the standards of a democratic society, because it is preferentially keeping its balances and checks on issues that require diplomatic management of perception rather than being the whistle blower and the voice of the truth.

PART II

Chapter VII

The U.S. Role in Future Mideast Policies

The collapse of the former Soviet Union and the termination of the politics of polarization between the West and the former USSR were supposed to result in a New Middle East. The strategic cooperation between Europe and the United States has partially dispersed uncertainty regarding security commitments in the Middle East. While the Iraq invasion successfully pushed the Arab-Israeli conflict to the backstage, new conflicts have emerged to engage U.S. policy makers in yet unprecedented power shows between Syria and Iran on one side and the Western world on the other side. Besides the circular negotiations between the West and the Syrian-Iranian axis, the struggle with Al-Qaeda, Hezbollah, and other Islamic groups in the Arab World and beyond remain major U.S. policy nightmares. In the absence of balanced powers in the world, which was particularly manifest in the politics of polarization between the "Western world" and the "Communist block," the global decision-making process has undergone a fundamental change. While the United Nations in general, and the Security Council in particular, were a playground for the superpowers to forge their policies and protect their interests during the cold war, the focus of the struggle for power and domination have changed. World politics is currently in chaos in the absence of a decisive decision-making process that enjoys worldwide respect in the White House. Institutions such as the World Bank, International Monetary Fund, World Trade Organization, and Transnational Organizations play, and/or are being used to design politics, in favor of funding countries. These institutions determine politics in certain parts of the globe and drive world economy under the banner of the globalization process. Amid globalization, the United States assumed a leading role that, due to its military and economic might, place it at the forefront of countries, which have to face international challenges. As a result of the role that the U.S. plays in world politics, both friends and foes of the U.S. in the Middle East variably charge the U.S. with almost every action in the region. Friends think that the U.S. could do more to help them eradicate the threat of Islamic terrorism, spread peace, and economically develop the region, while enemies, especially various Islamic groups, Syria, and Iran, accuse the U.S. of meddling in the affairs of the region and supporting Israel.

Strategic trade and economic blocks began to emerge in various parts of the world, including the Middle East. Deterrence and non-proliferation of weapons of mass destruction, combat of international terrorism, engagement of undemocratic and so-called rogue states and liberalization of world trade are central themes in the globalization process, which the U.S. leads. It was unthinkable just prior to the Camp David Accords of 1978 between Egypt and Israel that Arabs would sit face to face with the Israelis. Global changes should have a direct impact on the Middle East in constructive and positive ways. It is only a matter of time until peace takes place between Israel and more influential Arab states, including those of the Gulf region. However, the challenge will persist in the way peace can be transformed into reconciliation. The challenge is necessarily beyond the peace process. In the past, tensions and competition between major powers had aggravated local conflicts, but today, local politics is largely driven by the competition between the interests of world markets, mainly oil, combat of terrorism, and the desire to use the region as a playground to fight American and European influence. To turn wars into peace and peace into reconciliation, to transform conflicts into co-operation and enmity into partnership, to replace tension by stability, the Middle East region must adopt a comprehensive and fundamental change. The region falls in the heart of international wealth and constitutes a major and vital component of world economy; it is, therefore, understandable to witness widespread competition over its resources. The United States' policies in the Middle East stem largely from a traditional platform to defend the existence of Israel and keep the flow of oil. The political landscapes in the Middle East have dramatically changed, especially since 9/11 and the invasion of Iraq, to include the rise of Iran as a regional power at the helm of the Shiite Crescent, the spread of terrorism, and the primary struggle of Arab governments to keep terrorists and Islamists out of the government system. These changes necessitate a new U.S. foreign policy and the creation of new platforms upon which the U.S. must base its road map for good relations with the Middle East region for the next century. A new de-facto alliance is emerging between the anti-terror forces, which include the U.S., Europe, Israel, and the majority of Arab Muslims who vehemently denounce Bin Laden's Salafi strategy. Another dimension in this alliance is manifest in the collective Sunni Arab will to defeat Iran's emergence as a nuclear and regional Shiite power. The U.S. should capitalize on this rare opportunity in Middle East politics and work to bring the subtle allies into a strategic block to strengthen its presence in the region.

Many nations have extensive interests in the Middle East from the Gulf region and Iran along the Mediterranean coast to North Africa. Although every world power, throughout time, displayed willingness to go to war over the rich and strategic resources of the Middle East, the threats pending against the region remain largely local. To disperse and eliminate local threats, which are likely to be exacerbated by the showdown between extensive foreign interests and the struggle to fend off local terrorism from destabilizing the status quo, the Middle East should benefit from a wider Mediterranean experience and build a community. The countries of the region have a lot in common to form communities in every aspect of their existence. The security, welfare, status, prosperity, and existence of every Middle Eastern country should be treated as a collective interest towards the stability and harmony of the Middle East and the Mediterranean. Building a Mediterranean system is ultimately the creation of a regional community, which is capable of restoring and maintaining stability. A New Mediterranean is a system that should attempt to harmonize the interests of European states, the United States of America, and the rest of the world with those of Middle Eastern states. It should provide the region with grounds to compete globally as an effective partner with other world trade and economic blocs. Mediterraneanism is more than alliance and less than unity; it is a strategic partnership.

Chapter VIIII

A New Mediterranean

A New Mediterranean is the ultimate peace solution that transcends individual interests to embrace a broader regional and international initiative. Mediterraneanism is a simulation of the Southeast Asian strategic organizations such as APEC (Asia Pacific Economic Cooperation Forum) and ASEAN (Association of South East Asian Nations). It should constitute multiple novel institutions at all social, cultural, economic, environmental, legal, security, and strategic levels. Such a system should include all states geographically located along the coast of the Mediterranean Sea as well as other states that have social, economic, and security interests in the region. The European Union (EU) and the United States may contribute to the system as balancing members, since they have to operate from within other structural organizations and global commitments. Gulf and Arab states, including those of North Africa as well as Iran, Israel, and Turkey, may participate as full members. This region is strategically designated as the Mediterranean Crescent. Full participating member states contribute to all forums that comprise the system, while balancing members, which include the EU and the U.S., shall operate in the system to harmonize their interests with those of the region, provide technical support, and help to build confidence through their influence globally and regionally. Any forum that brings together U.S. and EU's interests with the strategic and security concerns of regional states is indispensable to peace, stability, and development. It should be mentioned, however, that although the problems of Southeast Asia are different than those of the Middle East, the partnership experiences of Southeast Asia, through ASEAN and APEC, are outstanding examples of co-operation and self-restraint in a volatile region. Unlike the situation with the EU, for instance, democracy was not a prerequisite to creation of regional associations in Southeast Asia. The democratic experience in the Mediterranean Crescent is likely to evolve through the exigencies and necessities facing the region, and with diligent effort by the EU and U.S., the strategic co-operation will certainly contribute to the evolution of democracy. The current situation in the Middle East requires engagement of all people to primarily face the challenge of local and international terrorism. A policy of inclusion, rather than containment, is capable of bearing constructive results even under circumstances where difficult ideologies drive the state and the political process. A new security and socio-economic structure in the Mediterranean Crescent, while still requiring the U.S. to take the lead role, has to be designed to take into account the changing will and abilities of regional states relative to each other and the U.S., and Europe. The architecture must not marginalize the existence of any nation and shall ensure an equal opportunity for all states regardless of their strategic and philosophical backgrounds. Policies such as deterrence and containment must be eliminated as central strategic themes, or approaches, in a modern structure of co-operation in the New Mediterranean. Friendly notions such as involvement, inclusion, engagement, and partnership should be advocated among all nations in the region. An attempt to reshape the strategic, economic, social, political, and military situations in the Mediterranean Crescent requires a thorough redefinition of its geopolitical structure. The region is central to international wealth, but it is strongly committed to religious teachings and historical determinants. Restructuring the regional governing regimes requires deep and serious consideration of its social concerns and mosaic. Imperialism of all kind had left enduring prints on the awareness of the people regardless of their religious, national, and philosophical descent. The influence of Iran on Islamic philosophies, the conflicts between the Islamists and Israel, the rise of fundamentalism and spread of terrorism, proliferation of weapons of mass destruction, and competition between world powers in the Mediterranean Crescent must be gradually dissipated through strategic and interlocking institutions.

A Mediterranean system is specially designed to take into account the potential of fast development of the region. It should promote the relationship between good governance, respects for human rights, and the rule of law, economic openness and fairness, and prospects for transforming the region into a "new economy" through education and technological advances. The system should also facilitate provision of social justice for all people and particularly minorities, which include Christians, Jews, Kurds, Armenians, etc. Understanding the vital interaction between political, economic, and social policies and security is a fundamental requirement for the building of a competitive and prosperous region. The history of all conflicts in the Mediterranean Crescent indicate that security in that part of the world has been, and is increasingly becoming, more of a social rather than a military base. Therefore, preservation and promotion of social peace through economic development and grass-root education will be crucial to stability. The New Mediterranean should guarantee regional co-operation and provide an ultimate peace solution, through which the United States and its European allies play a fundamental role in the democratization process of the Middle East. The democratization of the Middle East cannot be achieved by wars that gratify the need of terrorists and serve their purpose to recruit fighters and spread their ideologies, but, on the contrary, it is obtained through education and the spread of freedom and personal initiative regardless of the individual's ethno-religious denomination. This endeavor is a milestone that U.S. diplomats and policy makers should relentlessly work to actualize in order the protect America's strategic interests in the Middle East for many decades to come.

CHAPTER IX

Architecture of the New Mediterranean

The establishment of an economic development forum, or a regional economic confederation, with the main objectives to bring the region in line with the requirements and fluctuations of global economy is imperative. It is necessary to economically develop the Middle East in order to alleviate alienation at the grassroots level and prevent terrorists from penetrating local communities. This regional community can be achieved through compromise and reconcilement between regional, European, and American interests to fend off emerging global rivalries and maintain stability. A Mediterranean forum for economic co-operation and development should facilitate free market economy and deal with problems of fiscal policies, inflation, employment, management of natural and strategic resources, and the creation of a Mediterranean Monetary Fund (MMF). An American-European consent to develop and democratize the Mediterranean Crescent, along with a will among regional states to fund this forum, and in collaboration with international organizations such as the World Bank, are extraordinary foundations for its success. Economic prosperity and free trade must occupy a high priority for such a forum to pave the ground for the people to contribute to the democratization process of the region and keep the U.S. and its European allies harmoniously involved in a plan that can grant the transformation of the Middle East.

Agriculture is still by large the main source of living in the countries stretching along the southeastern zone of the Mediterranean Sea. The agricultural sector is widely primitive and in urgent need for modernization. Local governmental assistance is generally extensive in most countries, but collective and concerted regional initiatives are likely to revolutionize the sector and provide better living standards. Irrigation is the ultimate problem, and global warming is adding to this dilemma in an arid region, while new machinery and reliance on scientific crop techniques are subject to enormous improvement. Modernization of agriculture can be achieved through consolidation of knowledge and expertise among local countries, while the American and European experiences should facilitate the consolidation process and pave the way for foreign investors to contribute to an agricultural revolution in the Mediterranean Crescent. Agricultural produce markets are increasingly less accessible to small states amid intense competition between existing and emerging global trade blocs. The Mediterranean Crescent should develop its own trade entity, as part of a global trade system, in order to become capable of protecting the interests of local farmers. Collective regional strategies, based largely on reconcilement between the strategic approaches of individual states, can achieve that. Such a strategy consists of three fundamentals. Firstly, heavy dependence of local economies on agriculture requires protection of farmers' rights and amelioration of their living standards. This initiative should depend on financial aid to local farmers to go alongside assistance in other areas. Local governments and other aid groups such as the prospective Mediterranean Monetary Fund, the UN, and balancing members should provide financial aid. Secondly, eradication of agricultural primitiveness depends on modern machinery to revolutionize the sector and provision of necessary basic education to farmers through seminars and professional workshops designed by local research and scientific institutes. Development of the agricultural sector in the Middle East should be a lucrative market for American and European investors, with potential expansion for interested companies beyond the borders of individual states. Thirdly, the region should engage in a community commissioned to best configure protection of agricultural produce markets in an increasingly free global economy.

Global transformations require thorough consideration of what type of markets the region can afford. Ideologically driven policies of robust protectionism are repulsive to foreign investors and, especially in the Mediterranean Crescent, these policies constitute grounds for social tension. With the exception of a narrow proportion of agricultural products, the region is widely receptive for any kind of investment. Although full-fledged liberalization of local markets is impossible both on factual and logical grounds, reduction and/or gradual elimination of trade and tariff barriers are necessary. Investments in education, science, technology, the environment, health, the economy, and many other fields should create jobs and enhance the living standards of the local population. Investments are most likely to happen in an environment free of obstructionism. In light of the relative progress in liberalization of world trade, pressure is mounting on the region to stand on equal footings with the rest of the world. Free trade discussions and alternatives to compensate for losses as a consequence of adoption of new market philosophies can merge the region with current global transformations with relative ease. The establishment of such communities can be done at bi- and multilateral levels, while simultaneous establishment of other communities will help design a new and modern architecture for trade and investments in the region.

In spite of the fact that economic prosperity and investments are dominating governmental and intellectual spheres in modern diplomacy, upholding human values should not be a less important issue. Global philosophical divisions are becoming less relevant and gaps between capitalism, socialism, liberalism, and other schools of thought seem to be narrowing on practical, if not theoretical, grounds. Fundamental global issues like the environment, health, control of growth in the world population, crime, consolidation of democracies and upholding human rights, drug trafficking, and international terrorism are preoccupying decision makers and governments. The international struggle for the security and prosperity of humanity should not undermine the value of the human as an individual. Therefore, labor markets in the countries proposed to constitute the building blocs of the New Mediterranean must be regulated, and local governments should comply with the standards of worldwide labor market practices. A labor community should be established to involve government representatives, trade and labor unions, and investors at both local and regional levels in order to harmonize the interests, protect the rights, and appropriately regulate this sector. The building of a labor market community is tangible not only at a local level, but at multilateral and regional levels.

Proper exploitation of natural resources, potentials to generate electricity, and alternative sources of energy preserve both the wealth and environment of the region. Some oil producing countries in the Gulf and North Africa have refineries in neighboring countries to develop industries and generate jobs. The steady increase of population in the region will inevitably require greater demand for food supply, therefore, development and modernization of the agricultural sector and provision of effective irrigation systems should lead to increased output of food products. Fishery is a sector that should also be exploited in an environmentally friendly manner. Novel strategies should be developed to attract corporate investments and should be culturally tailored to market products in unique cultural and social environments. The U.S. role in such a regional architecture is paramount on technical and diplomatic grounds, since any U.S. involvement will engender a cultural development capable of serving America's long-term strategic interests.

The establishment of a Mediterranean Monetary Fund (MMF) is a vital initial step towards the initiation, continuation, and maintenance of a successful Mediterranean system. The fund will be the most effective means to provide fast and necessary financial assistance for the building and development of the region. As for all other projects in the system, the Fund can start with little and manageable projects, which can be realistically funded. The MMF should be able to attract initial funds from balancing members in the system: potential corporate investors, the World

Bank, and regional states. The Fund should work in collaboration with the World Bank, and must constitute a regional lobby for the sole purpose of attracting funds and investments into the region. The technical development of the system is conditional and contingent upon strategic planning and prioritization of projects, effective use of resources, and appropriate assessment of potential benefits. The system can gradually and slowly evolve from little to larger regional and multinational projects and is able to attract funds and be commissioned to manage existing funds through panels of experts, which should be composed of representatives from member states and should include financial, industry, government, and private sector experts. The U.S. and its European allies can play a role in laying the foundation of a systematic development and institutionalization of the Middle East in a manner consistent with their market and democratic ideals. Guidance and sincere involvement based on wise U.S. decision-making processes can provide the Middle East with economic and social grounds to establish permanent and long-lasting peace.

CHAPTER X

Security and Strategic Co-operation

Security in the Mediterranean Crescent is a priority, upon which stability rests. An association to prevent the dangers of proliferation of weapons of mass destruction, including nuclear, biological, and chemical is essential. Religious fundamentalism, terrorism, and extreme nationalism pose serious threats to regional stability and security. A security association is a phase of diplomacy that shall harness efforts by the region to combat common threats, especially terrorism. The security association should restlessly work to resolve existing and potential conflicts, preserve the independence, and protect sovereignty of all states by sincere diplomatic mediation. U.S. diplomacy has a long way to go on that path, which is one of the areas where every U.S. Administration seems to lack a road map that transcends partisan politics. The security of the Middle East is ultimately of great benefit to both the U.S. and EU's economy and stability.

Dissipation of fear and mistrust between the states of the Mediterranean Crescent is only possible through adoption of a common defense strategy that brings all states into one military alliance. Common defense creates new perception of the threats facing the region and the prospects of its development, prosperity, and harmony. Common defense eliminates Arab paranoia of Israel's military superiority, and assures Israel of Arab intentions to redirect their defense capabilities. A common defense strategy prevents the evolution of destabilizing military alliances, similar to the Syrian-Iranian axis, especially if the U.S. is even-handedly involved in regional security maintenance. The Shiite alliance between Syria, Iran, and Iraqi and Lebanese Shiites, constitutes major threats, especially in terms of arms race and proliferation of non-conventional weapons. A leading role by the U.S. and its European allies should undoubtedly strengthen the existence of such a co-operative strategic forum. A key step in the establishment of security co-operation is confidence building and the termination of U.S. strategy to ensure Israel's military superiority over the Arab states. U.S. policy makers have to conceptualize a better security measure to protect Israel and help absorb the changing will of the Arab population towards the Jewish State. Both Arabs and Israelis face a common threat, the spread of fundamentalism in their midst and use of terrorism to change the regional structure. The rise of Iran as a Shiite regional and potentially nuclear power is causing significant panic among the Sunnis and deepening the resistance of Hamas, Islamic Jihad, and Hezbollah against Israel's existence. Sunni Arabs perceive this new regional influence for Iran as an arson attack on their role to back and support a Sunni dominant Palestinian population. Sunni Arab states, especially Saudi Arabia, Egypt, and Jordan, which are most amenable to be part of a regional security arrangement that includes Israel, are cognizant that Iran hijacked the Palestinian cause through Islamism and made negotiations between Israel and the Palestinians very difficult. These moderate Arab states, in addition to the Gulf countries, North Africa, and Lebanon, will not hesitate to be part of a regional security association that is whole-heartedly backed by the U.S. at the military and diplomatic levels. Both Jordan and Egypt signed peace treaties with Israel, while Saudi Arabia maintains a subtle position that facilitates peace negotiations between Arabs and Israelis. However, the situation that Syria and Iran created in the Palestinian territories and Lebanon, through Hamas and Hezbollah, respectively, not only sabotaged the will for negotiation but gave Iran and the Shiite greater influence to fight U.S. Mideast policies.

Military and strategic planning in individual states should be brought in line with the general strategy of a wider regional system, in which the U.S. should have an integral role. Strategic and military strategies should change focus from national defense against bordering countries to maintenance of regional stability through a forum that must concentrate its efforts on regional inter-state relations. Security planning should primarily include containment of media escalation of social, racial, and sectarian tension, while the military should earn credibility in strategic planning to change the attitude of the military from a "war machine" and/or "tool of oppression" to a strategic defense sector. Therefore, drafting research and education programs that target military schools will help create new perception and self-esteem of military personnel.

Education and training programs do not necessarily have to be on military and strategic issues but should create willingness and an ideology to make military institutions an integral part of the development strategy of the region. A twofold strategy should be delegated to this community: firstly, to render military institutions part of the economic and scientific evolution of the region, and secondly, to train the military to protect national and regional security. The establishment of a "security community" should foster an understanding within the military that economic prosperity, institutionalization, good neighborly relations, and capabilities of national defense are an integrated perspective. This understanding is a vital element on the path of popular "image building" for the military.

Regional co-operation will help the Middle East explore venues and discover means to strengthen relations with the world. Despite the diverse cultural, social, and religious fabric of the region, all countries incorporated in the New Mediterranean should look upon themselves as an "anatomical strategic entity." Foreign relations between the countries of the region and the rest of the world must be co-ordinated to preserve regional security and stability. Joint regional ventures to build trade, defense, and foreign relations outside the region will gradually be based on common strategic planning and consultation. A regional forum for strategic and foreign relations should conduct education programs that promote an infrastructure, which should provide bi- and multilateral dialogues to gradually formulate common foreign relations policies, in which the U.S. and Europe have effective role.

Peace is a result of interrelated factors whose existence, or non-existence, can impinge on social harmony in the region. It is essential to grasp the transformation in the world and the ubiquitous walk away from the cold war style of attitude toward security. A novel security architecture in the Middle East should take into account transformation of focus from the military to "informed" diplomacy. Peace deals between Israel and Arab countries are inevitably subject to time, while the security, cultural perspectives, and the economy of Turkey are relatively dependent on the region. The challenges are eventually beyond the peace process between the Arabs and Israelis; they are embedded in the way peace can be just and comprehensive and the platform that should turn peace into genuine reconciliation. Security and peace can be maintained through high levels of dialogue and discussions, including attainment of regional consensus to build a common defense strategy, which should be founded on careful appreciation of the common threats facing the region. The spread of weapons of mass destruction, combat of terrorism, prevention of sectarian fundamentalism, and natural resources, especially water, are the most flammable factors in the Mediterranean Crescent. The deliberate expression of mutual understanding, respect for the sovereignty, and independence of others must reinforce the security strategy. Armed forces' visits and participation in joint military exercises at multilateral levels will build mutual confidence, on which security depends. Furthermore, sharing intelligence and holding talks on regional security and development should constitute the driving force of strategic military planning and concepts.

Proliferation of weapons of mass destruction remains the most threatening factor to peace and stability in the Middle East. This dilemma has to be approached in a global rather than a regional or local strategy. Many regional states are known to develop programs of non-conventional weapons, the most frightening of which is Iran's political and popular ambition to develop a Shiite nuclear bomb to counter Israeli military superiority and challenge the U.S.-

European will. Confidence building, particularly between military institutions, and co-operation at the economic, social, and other levels are likely to minimize the difficulties of containing proliferation of weapons of mass destruction. The region must become a target for international conferences and conventions on proliferation of weapons of mass destruction, with education campaigns to highlight the implications of these weapons. Involvement of the G-8 countries and the UN is instrumental in the success of such initiatives, which should primarily aim at bringing people face to face for dialogue and negotiations. Provision of incentives for the region, in terms of technical and financial assistance, will build more confidence between the U.S. and its foes. Confidence building is contingent upon cessation of media campaigns that aggravate problems and build tension. There ought to be softer expressions and constructive attitudes, across the global and regional spectrum to describe foreign policies and approaches to other nations.

CHAPTER XI

Mediterranean Human Rights

The success of strategic common defense and adoption of free market economies in the Mediterranean Crescent are contingent upon respect for the human rights, territorial sovereignty, and political independence of all states. The establishment of a Mediterranean justice system to adjudicate and arbitrate in regional conflicts and breaches of human rights and international law is both compelling and compassionate. The justice system should operate according to the recommendations of international law and various organizations of the United Nations. Respect for human rights is a major step towards the gradual democratization and institutionalization of the Mediterranean Crescent. The creation of a regional Court for Justice requires courage and determination by both the people and states of the region. Human rights are best attained through education and institution building measures. Injustices are the underpinnings of poverty, instability, and social and political disorder in the Middle East region. A Mediterranean Court for Justice shall constitute a panel of legal experts, lawyers and judges from all member states, including full and balancing members, and must adjudicate on issues that hold the system and cement it together. This court should be the supreme legal power in allocating resources if disagreements arise between member states, and must codify and formulate its laws and rules in collaboration with existing communities. The evolution of a regional court for justice should be based on the codes and practices formulated by various communities and must be assisted by inputs of international law and experience from balancing members. The court can start at bilateral levels and expand memberships to other states as they become ready to participate in the new strategic architecture of the region.

Creation of a new "individual" of the Mediterranean Crescent should mainly be the preoccupation of a specific regional institution devoted to human rights and education. Raising the awareness of the average population about the benefits of civil societies and institutions should bring about social renaissance to the region. The struggle for sectarian, tribal, and cultural supremacy is a ravaging tendency against the recognition of the individual. Civil and human rights are best obtained through institution building, such as social welfare organizations, civil societies, and professional clubs and associations, which should be steadily developed to release the average person from the tight grip of systematic alienation that plagues certain societies in the Middle East. The United States has many roles to play in this arena, including the provision of government grants that contribute to enhancement of civil rights and societies and promotion of multicultural peace. The U.S. State Department and other government organizations, including USAID, provide millions of dollars each year towards the development of small projects to promote harmony and understanding between the U.S. and the Middle East. U.S. government programs must be expanded to re-invent the region both culturally and educationally in order for the grassroots to push for their own civil and human rights through solid organizations.

Operation of the Mediterranean system should ensure, to the greatest possible extent, that no group or individual is disadvantaged. Social renaissance requires recognition of good ideas, so local communities or organizations must build connections with international venues specialized in the promotion of human and civil rights. Individual states should establish their own human rights and democracy institutes, which should thoroughly research the political, economic, social, and cultural elements that violate human rights and hinder democracy. Member states should delegate local activists, government and civil institutions, as well as military personnel to promote human rights in a regional forum. The ultimate goal would be to look at the recommendations on civil and human rights and develop education programs that transcend the region to involve balancing members. Education programs should include workshops on human rights, seminars for government and non-government personnel, reception of regional and international conventions, and promotion of the benefits of democracy through institution building and their role in the application of law. The United States and its European allies have a fundamental interest to promote justice and peace in the Middle

East, since that will not only reflect on their genuine efforts for democracy beyond their national borders, but also will deflect enormous pressure form that part of the world on the U.S. and Europe. Justice, civil, and human rights are core values of Western societies, and their extrapolation to the Middle East is both a moral and strategic victory.

Chapter XII

Education Is the Backbone of Development

Global struggle to reduce poverty and save the environment will continue to be lost unless current economic and social trends in the world's poor and developing countries are changed. Education is the way out of poverty and the foundation for human development and economic prosperity. Education is a universal benefit, not only useful to eradicate poverty and prevent mass alienation, but also essential for informed discussions and understanding. Member states of the Mediterranean Crescent must embrace education as a vital necessity. The Middle East region is expected to see more abject poverty, environmental damage, political instability, economic uncertainty, ethnic violence, religious fundamentalism, and terrorism if present social trends continue. The majority of regional conflicts boil down to social rather than military concerns, and it is only by education that social harmony and understanding can be fostered. For example, population growth is an alarming issue in some countries of the region, where in Egypt alone almost one million new birth cases are reported every year. Population growth in the Middle East in general, and among Muslim communities in particular, has serious repercussions within a global system, where lack of education seems to underlie many of the problems associated with it. It is projected that the world population will reach about nine billion by 2050, while half of the six billion people on Earth still live on less than two dollars a day. Two billion are not connected to any energy system and 1.5 billion lack clean water. More than a billion lack basic education, health care or modern birth control methods. Additionally, although some countries have made substantial progress on the road of basic development, a UN report on literacy in the Arab world has shown that more than 90 percent of women are illiterate and lack basic education. During the last decade, reading of newspapers increased from 52 to 82 kilograms per one thousand people in Europe and decreased from 3.3 to 2.7 kilograms per one thousand people in the Arab world. These social and cultural trends undermine societal progress and severely limit the spread of education, which seems to be the only means to deliver people form poverty, economic hardships, and political alienation.

A systematic promotion of education can largely be achieved through a Mediterranean forum that operates restlessly to wrestle the ravaging cultural and social epidemic of illiteracy and lack of education. Besides basic education, the forum should promote awareness of environmental politics, ensure primary education for children, and eliminate discrimination against women. It should also bridge the "digital divide" and stimulate the development and assimilation of information technology by bringing the Internet to schools, libraries, hospitals, social clubs, and government and non-government services. Education is mandatory to democracy and the rule of law, because democracy can only be conceived of, and stimulated, through education and its unlimited social, cultural, and economic benefits. Education is the starting point for the development and transformation of the Mediterranean Crescent into a knowledge-region. Regional conflicts are, indeed, mainly driven by lack of understanding of the historical, cultural, religious, and social backgrounds, which facilitate harmony and coexistence among people. Education creates new perceptions and different views of the world, so it offsets political instability, religious fundamentalism, and sectarian violence, and promotes communication and consensus on common interests.

The establishment of education and a technology community must work at both the basic and advanced levels of education. Social and economic developments require eradication of illiteracy among the overwhelming majority of population, and especially women. Adult education programs are mandatory to provide basic education to the illiterate population and schemes of continuing education for early school-leavers and the middle-aged. Integration of education and industry through professional and industrial workshops and training programs must assist in the development of industries. Access to knowledge and education must be permanent, and local libraries and newspapers should prevent the alienation of remote and poor population and provide grounds for wider contribution to a successful and comprehensive regional evolution. Education at the basic level is necessary to provide grounds for a knowledge-based region and scopes for advanced technology and indispensable expertise. International aid agencies, the World Bank, the United Nations, and member states of the system must have keen interests in such a human development.

At more sophisticated levels of the educational revolution, introduction of computer and scientific technology into schools and universities, computerization of services, and joint education programs between locals and foreign experts are commendable for a modern and employable education. In the tertiary education arena, joint scientific research programs, sharing university curricula, and structuring courses and materials about foreign and regional countries should widen the scope of knowledge and promote mutual understanding between the people. Each country in the Mediterranean Crescent should make maximum profit of the Internet to minimize distances, improve communication, and educate the local population. Internet in each school, hospital, university, and business will bring popular awareness about the rest of the world and assist in a much faster development of the region. Trade of knowledge and expertise through cooperation and joint regional and international ventures must attract more funds for education and development. Above all, provision of education, establishment of research programs, and adoption of technology must stop the ongoing brain drainage in the Middle East. It is the brain and intellectual drainage that opens the way wide for the fundamentalists to brain wash people and turn them against the U.S. Promotion of education is the most effective long-term strategy that is able to bridge cultural gaps, counteract the clash of civilizations, and provide an alternative peaceful means for democratization and harmony in the region.

The region should not only accustomize to the application of knowledge, but it must also pursue knowledge and build its own wealth of it. Scientific research at the industry level is necessary in the farming, health, and environmental sectors. Promotion of research is vital towards the establishment of a knowledge-based region. The research sector has now been recognized worldwide as a cornerstone in national economic prosperity and international competitiveness. Programs and advertising campaigns should be designed to promote and highlight the benefits of education and the search for knowledge at all levels. Joint university programs both within the region and beyond, with Europe, the U.S., Canada, Australia and Japan, and provision of short-term scholarships for scholars and researchers will increase regional creativity and co-operation. Such programs will also harmonize relations and strengthen bonds within the region and with the world. Scientific cooperation may start at a very modest scale, but it is likely to attract foreign corporations and investors to develop a research sector of a universal benefit. Available regional wealth should be used to develop and modernize alternative foundations for strong and competitive national economies. That experience has already been witnessed in Saudi Arabia and the United Arab Emirates, where a drastic and strategic change took place from heavy reliance on oil to adoption of worldwide services, tourism, agricultural development, and other forms of trade. This partial walk away from reliance on oil and development of other economic means of national growth is a strategic policy for the U.S., whose economy depends heavily on Middle Eastern oil. The contribution of the U.S. and Europe to conduce the oil-rich Middle Eastern states to ubiquitously rely on economic revenues separate from oil rests squarely on education that grants the local population international recognition and competitiveness. The U.S. possesses powerful means to promote education in the region and exchange military spending for long-term investment in educational programs at all basic, technological, and tertiary levels.

High technology to promote effective corporate governance, banking regulations, and accounting standards must be training areas for the educated population. More efforts to develop the so-called "new economy," which is based on investments in the high technology sector, are also essential. The potential of the Middle East to float its resources and potential technology and research innovations on the world stock and financial markets is enormous. Nevertheless, local banking and financial sectors must be radically restructured in most countries to become more hospitable to foreign investments. Integration of high technological advances and financial markets require highly concerted and co-operative regional initiatives to compete with giant world economic powers. The high-tech revolution must enable the region to link its services locally and internationally and achieve an economic and trade bloc integral to the global economy. Therefore, a number of areas for potential governmental and corporate investments exist in order for the U.S. to benefit from a major peace that can transform the Middle East and provide long-term outcomes for America's involvement in the Mediterranean Crescent.

Chapter XIII

The Environment and Natural Resources

The preservation of the environment and exploitation of natural resources according to friendly and strategic management programs should be a regional venture. The region cannot escape global environmental challenges, including global warming, cleanliness of drinking water, protection of the earth's forests, contamination of the soil, search for alternative clean and renewable energy sources, and preservation of aquatic habitats and wildlife. The importance of the environment is integral to generation of wealth and provision of safe and secure habitats for all living things. An alarming natural threat in the Mediterranean Crescent today is the steadily declining level of rainfall, with strong indication that the region is heading into the driest era ever in history. The local population tells about drying natural water sources, and a report by the United Nations on the Middle East showed that if rainfall levels continue on the decline the region would face complete drought by the year 2020. The recommendations of the 1997 Kyoto Protocol on the management of Greenhouse effects and global warming constitute another reason for concern. An international panel of scientists appointed to look at the trend of global warming after the Kyoto Protocol affirmed that the temperature of the earth would increase between one and five degrees Celsius over the next century. Regardless of the current international and scientific debate about global warming, water, which is naturally the scarcest resource in the Middle East, needs to be harnessed and managed properly to meet environmental, industrial, urban, irrigation, and electricity requirements. The scarcity of water has transformed it from a substance of life to a motif of conflict in the region, where many wars are fought over water sources. Conflicts such as the Israeli-Syrian in the Golan Heights over the Tebriah lake, the Lebanese-Syrian and Lebanese-Israeli disagreements over the

Assi and Litani rivers, respectively, and the Syrian-Turkish and Syrian-Iraqi tension over the Euphrates and Tigris rivers, are major long-term conflicts based on water resources. Water management is not only necessary to resolve conflicts and secure stability but also to provide useful assets for the economy, agriculture, and tourism, therefore, existing and potential water resources should be harnessed and exploited to meet the challenges of global warming and environmental damage. Turkey, Iraq, and Egypt are among existing regional powers, which have abundant water resources from the Tigris, Euphrates, and Nile Rivers. Building dams for irrigation and clean drinking water based on regional arrangements to offset environmental challenges is necessary to increase water and food supply, while recreational facilities alongside the dams are valuable economic revenues. In addition, scientific methods will enable the region to continue to expand the desalination of seawater in the Gulf States, Israel, Syria, Jordan, and elsewhere. The water shortage challenge is the most urgent to face in order to prevent future famine, economic uncertainty, poverty, and political instability in the volatile Mediterranean Crescent.

Lebanon tops the list of regional countries as a water reservoir that has potential to embark on a so-called "engineering wonder" of the twenty-first century. The snow remains on Lebanese mountains across the year, while most of the snowmelt water escapes to the sea. Lebanon, for example, can benefit from the Australian experience of the Snowy Mountains Hydro-Electric Scheme, which revolutionized Australian clean energy supply and provided agricultural land, industries, and urban Australia with reliable water supplies. The construction of the scheme spun for twenty-five years, during which Australia was fully committed to a period of economic growth. The scheme was constructed after World War II and helped absorb about 100,000 workers, of whom two thirds came from war-torn Europe. The project helped Australia recover its war losses and build a resilient and relatively immune economy after the war. In addition to what the Snowy Mountains Hydro-Electric Scheme produces in terms of water and energy, it is a relatively environmentally friendly project and a valuable economic asset for Australia. The scheme produces clean renewable energy equivalent to five million tons of carbon dioxide emissions every year. It provides irrigation reservoirs of 2,360 gigaliters (1 gigalitre is equal to 1,000,000,000 liters) of water and generates 5,100 gigawatt hours (1 gigawatt equals 1,000,000 kilowatts) of renewable electricity annually. Furthermore, most of the engineering features of the scheme (four power stations, 145 km of interconnecting tunnels, and 80 km of aqueducts) are located underground and attract a great deal of corporate interest and expertise. The scheme is also a hot tourism spot and an investment that will last Australia for hundreds of years. In the light of the Australian experience, Lebanon can undergo radical reform of its strategic national and economic assets to recover from a mountain of national debts, foster social and multi-communal unity, and stop a deadly flow of emigration and brain drainage, especially among the youth. A hydroelectric scheme will totally reverse the current Lebanese situation and help Lebanon become the power generator for a considerable part of the region. The scheme is a candidate to absorb youth energy, establish potential national unity, and provide economic prosperity for decades to come. The expertise needed and the workforce necessary to build such a scheme will help Lebanon retain its youth and resolve its unemployment dilemma. The scheme may also attract expatriate Lebanese, who have left Lebanon for economic and security reasons. Most importantly, Lebanon will be unable to achieve such a giant project on its own, so it will need regional and international assistance in terms of technology and expertise, workforce, money, and ideas. Therefore, while a hydroelectric scheme on Lebanese mountains is a rationale to collect, store, and divert water for irrigation, urban use, and generation of electricity, it will also help Lebanon head off threats of drought and become a strategic regional power to be accounted for. Water is one of Lebanon's most abundant and important natural resources, which, if exploited promptly, will revolutionize the country's economy. Lebanon is likely to witness an oversupply of water and power as a result of the project, so both water and power will constitute a trade commodity for the economy. The scheme will provide invaluable recreational assets and will attract international and regional corporate investments into the country. The case of Lebanon is another vivid example of U.S. potentials to invest in the Middle East and develop the region and put it on the road of peace, while advancing domestic strategic and economic aims.

Besides natural resources, history is embedded in every stone and manifest in every town of the Mediterranean Crescent. The depth and significance of history, the cultural and religious diversity of the region, and the uniqueness of its environment should be combined to make it one of the hottest spot of tourism in the world. However, two factors deter tourists from exploring the elegance of the Mediterranean Crescent, terrorism, and limitation of movement between countries due to conflicts and political instability. The differences in the cultural fabric of the region can be bridged via creation of a common interest for all. For instance, it is always a fascination for foreign tourists to see an environment different from their homeland, explore the cultural diversity of the region, and observe the landmarks of thousands of years of history and civilizations. A tourism project can be implemented to create wealth from history that links the historical landmarks of the region via safe recreational routes, making a holiday in the Mediterranean Crescent very interesting and inspiring. Tourists can start their journey in Egypt and explore the biblical, architectural, and historical significance of the Pyramids and then proceed either to North Africa or Jerusalem and Bethlehem to walk on the land that gave birth to Judaism, and Christianity. From Jerusalem, the route continues to Jericho and Amman in Jordan and on to Iraq and Baghdad, one of the most historically significant cities of the region. In Iraq tourists explore the sites of successive civilizations of Mesopotamia, including Babylonians and Assyrians, etc., and the Hanging Gardens of Babylon. The route can continue in three different directions, either towards Byzantine and Ottoman landmarks in Turkey and Istanbul, or Iran and the Gulf and Holy Cities of Mecca and Medina of Saudi Arabia, where a trip is an invigorating exploration of Muslim culture and traditions. Alternatively, the route from Jerusalem can lead into Lebanon's historical cities of Tyre, Sidon, Beirut, and Byblos and into Syria to explore the archaeological sites along the Canaanite and the Phoenician coasts, which witness ten thousand years of active human history. Byblos is the birthplace of the alphabet, which was formulated and codified by the Phoenicians in 800 B.C. Inland tourists can enjoy the scenes of the snowy mountains and head into the Bekaa Valley, which was known as the winery and the warehouse of the Roman Empire. In the Bekaa, the ruins of Baalbeck constituted the eastern border of the Roman Empire and the ruins of Anjar are vivid manifestations of the Omayates and Arab rules. From the Bekaa, the travel distance to Damascus is less than an hour. Damascus is an historical city and known as the Throbbing Heart of Arabism. In Syria tourists can visit many religious and historical sites and proceed inland to Iraq and Jordan. The routes that link the historical and cultural landmarks of the region can be constructed either as safe highways or express railways. In rural areas, recreational facilities can be built alongside routes to bring prosperity to remote regions. The project should enable the region to find common economic and cultural interests and help transform history from a base of conflict into a melting pot of economic and strategic cooperation and coexistence. U.S. and European companies and governments can play an indispensable role in the economic and strategic development of the New Mediterranean. Foreign contribution will be that of peaceful development and economic gain rather than forceful strategies. Besides history, the environment can be used to attract tourists, as a light plane or express train only takes a few hours from either the Sinai or Arabian Deserts to the snowy Lebanese mountains and the beautiful beaches on the Mediterranean Sea. The Mediterranean Crescent holds promising developments based on the treasures that environmental, social, cultural, and historical diversity have imparted on it.

Putting It in Perspective

The ultimate peace is the work of multiple governments to protect the Middle East from the spread of terrorism and danger of religious fundamentalism. Peace is a regional multifaceted venture that should take into account the danger of rising powers and their influence on the region's Islamic population. The rules of engagement must change and the U.S. should help build partnerships that not only enhance U.S. standing and credibility in the region but also contribute to confidence building among the local population. U.S. policy makers have a unique and unprecedented opportunity to take advantage of the subtle alliances that emerged in the region post 9/11 and as a result of the fall of Saddam Hussein's regime and the rise of Iran as a regional power at the helm of the Shiite crescent. The U.S. can benefit and substantially contribute to the advancement of its own interests in the Middle East if the incumbent and future administrations really master the strategic use of political dexterity in the region. A fundamental step towards permanent peace that can result in regional development and partnership is the establishment of a New Mediterranean based on the recognition of the importance of confidence building. Confidence can be generated by face to face discussions, joint ventures, and education programs that will enable the region to understand and appreciate its position in the world and vice versa. The success and integration of a regional system, in which the U.S. plays a leading role, are best achieved through creation of sets of regional interlocking institutions to facilitate political debate and generate strategic links between the member states. The best way for the U.S. and its allies to play a role in the establishment of a strategic system in the Middle East is to be involved in the development of communities that are able to oppose extremist ideologies and fight terrorism and religious fundamentalism at its cradle. The system should be put in place to help the region stand at equal footings with the rest of the world and protect its building blocs from marginalization by the pressing globalization process. The amalgamation of regional resources and expertise will assist in the fast and necessary development, while the U.S. and Europe play a role that might lead to harmony and peace. It is insufficient to speak of a peace process when the challenges lie far beyond peace negotiations. A New Mediterranean is an ultimate peace solution that will enable the U.S. to engage the local population and institutionalize, harmonize, reconcile, and recover the Middle East from wars and conflicts, which dominated all aspects of life in it since time immemorial. This system will constitute a platform for the U.S. to base its policies for decades to come, as a stable Middle East means less terrorism against America, international security, and constant flow of oil. Additionally, the U.S. will be able to forge its policies through collective forums, which include several regional states. It is an opportunity for the U.S. to take advantage of the geo-political changes in the Middle East and transform them into permanent social trends capable of enlightening the region and moving its people against the brainwashing machine of religious fundamentalism and anti-Americanism.